I0623806

QUIET UNDERPINNINGS

Aleathia Drehmer

ROADSIDE PRESS

Quiet Underpinnings
Copyright © Aleathia Drehmer 2026
ISBN: 979-8-9996256-6-3
Library of Congress Control Number: 2026933128

All rights reserved. No part of this text may be used or reproduced in any manner without written permission from the author or publisher except in the case of brief quotations embodied in critical articles and reviews.

Editor: Michele McDannold
Cover Art: Anastasiya Fluegel

Roadside Press
Meredosia, Illinois

For my father—thank you for the love of the outdoors, for the gift of silence and listening, and for all of your quiet love.

I miss you.

For Chris—there is no greater adventure than the ones we share together. Thank you for always indulging my endless curiosities.

I love you.

This collection was written over a three year period and is based on the Japanese understanding of living in 72 microseasons. This means that each of these poems was written within the microseason itself which is 4-5 days long. There are 24 larger seasons and each of those contains three poems.

Table of Contents

Grid of Civilization 1

The Smell of Earth...2

Totem Rising..3

Connected 5

Surrender..7

Unattainable Heights 8

I Come Here to Stand Witness 9

a small girl blooms in the line at the patisserie.....................11

Food For Another Time 12

Threads 14

Descent..17

Ritual of Transition 19

There Are Still Mountains To Climb 20

Subtle Movements..21

Awakening..22

We..23

All the Empty Nests are Filled with Hope............................24

We Write Our Own Ending to the Story 25

Sleeping In...26

Innocent Pride..27

Underground Silence...28

Quiet Underpinnings...29

Life is Improvisation 31

Summer's Teeth 32

I'll Meet You At The River...34

I Still Keep Reaching 36

Never Get Old...38

Kiss Me When You Get Home 39

Summer Violet 40

Sitting on the Curb, Independence Day 41
Between the Lines We Find a Glimpse of Truth 42
The Mystery of Her Smile 44
No Hesitation 46
Manipulating Time 47
The Kind of Summer 48
All the Secrets 49
Disconnected 50
We Will Teach Each Other 51
Glowing Eyes 53
Dragonflies 54
The Memory of Summer 55
Where The Mud Opens Up to the River 56
Warm Air Rising 57
Harbingers of Rain 58
Humanness 59
The Silence of Easiness 61
This Age of Spontaneous Combustion 62
Banging on the Door 63
Hope Lake 64
Silent House 65
A Future Promise 66
The Rich Stuff 67
The Flaw 68
Unexpected 69
The Truth of Everything 70
Until My Breath is No More 71
Fire On The Mountain 72
Friendsgiving 73
Quiet Optimism 74
The Shift 75

Monochrome 76

As Snow 77

Holding Space 79

Self-Heal 80

Balance 81

Unpredictable 82

The Creek 83

Creature of Habit 85

The Future in a Drop of Dew 86

A Pain So Deep 87

Accumulate 88

Outstretched Hand 89

Publication Notes 90

About the Author 91

Grid of Civilization

The ancients believed
this was the time
when spring winds begin
to thaw the ice winter built
around us, but those were times
when the footprint of man
did more to create than destroy.

From the window, I stare out
across the land—built up with homes
and criss-crossing wires, this grid
of civilization, destruction.

Winds pelt against this old house—
standing over one hundred years,
watching man terraform wider
swathes of unnatural habitat.

The wind is so cold
the thermometer drops below zero,
so cold I hear the ancients cry
over what we've done
in the name of status and money,
and I wonder if spring
will ever show her face again.

The Smell of Earth

The air gives us sips of spring—
a taste of hope and the dexterity
of mother nature.

We walk our land, building imaginary
gardens behind us, dreams
planting themselves.

The idea of self-sustaining is not
a notion we want to keep
locked away inside a box.

Our bodies feel alive
after the heavy blanket
of winter is lifted, our fingers
digging deep in soil, the smell
of earth rising to make us smile.

We see starlings in their murmuration—
dancing across blue skies, harvesting
insects just awakening, and for a moment

I think I hear the nightingale sing,
a whisper evaporating in the sun.
He holds my hand, its warmth
invigorating and grounding, before
we drink in the last of the evening.

Totem Rising

I drive over the river, pass frozen ponds
knowing winter pushes its coldest water
to the surface, leaving warm pools
against the murky bottom we never see.

There, the fish have buried themselves
in soft sediment, hearts beating imperceptibly,
sleek scaled bodies alive with wisps of oxygen,
twitching slightly when the water finds vibrations.

Today I decided to quit fighting the season,
leaning into the cold emptiness
and hoping I'll be able to clutch my way
back out when the earth begins to thaw.

On the highway, my car hurtles through
the landscape made up of bleak gray and white,
this month nothing more than monochrome
colors bleeding into me with so much force.

A red-tailed hawk glides across the asphalt
lighting on a road sign. I say hello with my eyes,
the brick of his feathers standing out like an ember.
I think of my father, his soul forever trapped inside birds.

Then a dead hawk on the side of the road
signaling a loss of freedom and independence.

Then a dead fox on the side of the road
signaling the pain of growth and the space of grief.

Then another red tail hawk, very much alive,
Its presence is about focus and patience and determination.

Then, nothing.

The world slips back into its gray skirt,
but the memory of banded brick feathers
and tangerine fur, linger like sun spots in my eyes.

An invisible totem is rising from the earth
with the spirits of my ancestors singing,
hands covered in dirt and sky and wind.

Connected

It's unusually quiet in the forest
except for a few birds calling alert,
a brief reminder that I am an invader
in this world. A brief reminder
that my father has followed me here.
Both of us are connected in this solitude
where there is never a need for words.

The sun stretches her wings,
makes the snow sparkle
in the untouched places.
The crust is hard and slippery
from a path well traveled
by man and dog. Occasionally,
my boots sink and disappear.

Warmth nudges the underground,
alive even in a world of hibernation.
Thawing water searches for an opening,
for its full breadth of the season.
I hear the snow melting underfoot,
its subtle shift and crack like a whisper
from a lover who tells me I am everything
and for that moment, I let myself believe it.

In the places the earth reveals itself,
colored in the remnants of autumn,
it shows me where the creeks will run
in a month. This trail soon to be impassible
without sinking and sliding in deep mud.
The squelch of boots is a sound I've grown to love.

I'm overtaken on the trail by two sleek dogs
and their master hurrying to catch up—

calling ahead that they are both friendly.
The puppy sidles up to me with hesitation
and I notice her missing eye. I put my hand out
and the stump of her tail wags. The remaining
ice blue eye looks at me with a trust I've not earned.

Her coat is silky and silver like mercury
and I feel the life beneath her skin
like I do under the snow. The man tells me
she's a rescue and pulls her muddy paws
off my legs. We say good day and he calls
the puppy from me
                        Freyja, come. Freyja.
she bounds away as if I never existed.

I think about how apt her name is for she will fight
for everything. Inside her will be a magic
for seeing the future. Her singular eye opening
to the heavens, to the world, to us all.

This notion passes and melds into the fact
that I have no memories of my father in winter
except the ones I make with him now and how
our time together only folded us close in the arms
of the world as it arrived and said goodbye,
but never in its transition to death.

When I recognize this, birds break into their songs.
I stop to listen, taking in this place I've come to,
to prove something about myself, to myself,
and know that this is somehow my purpose.

Surrender

I sit at the table and watch the sun rise
into the gray, hazy sky. It's still winter
despite my heart wishing for spring.

The cats post on either side of me like sentry
or like studious mathematicians trying
to calculate the harmonic mean of us.

I hear my adult child stir upstairs, text her
that we are going walking and to dress warmly.
I failed to give her a chance to say no.

On the walking path we share ourselves
in a way that feels different. The cold air
stinging our cheeks and sharpening our breath

into a type of surrender that I long for.
It is here our steps fall into rhythm except
when dodging refrozen strands of ice

that formed like stunted, forgotten rivers
after several days of false spring
had its way with the land. The green

revealing itself, teasing us. Here we talk
like adults, like friends who have known
each other intimately for a lifetime.

This is a beauty that was never afforded to me,
my feet a simple metronome for a song
no one else would ever get to hear. But now

we are building a song together with footfalls
and ragged breath and the musicality of words
and there is no other place I'd rather be.

Unattainable Heights

I told myself I would only write these poems
outside, out in the world with my hands clutching
the seasons like oxygen, but here I am watching
the sunlight dance
        through the tall pines in my neighbors yard,
        through the torn screen leftover from the cat's youth,
        through the dirty window covered in paw prints and nose
boops,
onto the walls painted like the greenest grass.

Yesterday was another day of false spring,
the air warm and fresh with the idea of beginnings.
This morning I woke up to a chill
with another layer of snow on the ground.
I know it won't be enough to stop the buds
forming on trees or the early flowers
waiting for their cue to hit the stage.

I set my coffee on the ledge and lock the cats out.
I want this moment for myself
        as I watch the light sparkle against the new snow,
        as I watch the birds returning and know I will curse
          their predawn cacophony soon enough,
        as I watch clouds slowly drift across the powder blue sky
and think of my mother—her eyes the color of unattainable heights.

I try not to cry into my cup at the sentimental
return of light and warmth and green. It waits impatiently
inside my heart, its vibration is almost too much to handle.
But the clouds take the sun back from me
and the room falls into shadow. I take my cup
and go back into the life I've built and wait for spring.

I Come Here to Stand Witness

The air is bitter with wind,
pulling at my skin with icy hooks
as the sky lay deceptive with its
deep-oxygen blue and cotton clouds.
The sun spills out in waves
leaving me in phantom shadows,
but I know the world is waking up.

Songbirds have returned
and swoop over the high
muddy river now burgeoning
from unseasonable rains.
Mallards float backward
with the current, geese call
their obnoxious warning
as I crest the top of the dike
and come into view.

By the river, the long grass is matted,
slicked over with olive green river silt.
I scale down the embankment and cross paths
with a woodchuck emerging from his winter slumber.
The warmth signaling the return
of all things forgotten under the snow.

I stop and take it all in,
water and mud swirling around my boots,
and I couldn't be happier.

I quietly wonder if the queen bees
have begun to climb to the surface
to build her armies and lay eggs
before she fades into her own death
taking her most faithful with her.

She leaves an empire in her image.
She births a small nation.

This world constantly evolves
in waves of minutiae, its vibration
imperceptible and quiet. But I come
here to stand witness. I come here
to behold and to be held by a life
I'd once taken for granted.

a small girl blooms in the line at the patisserie

cold white snow on ground
world waits for cherry blossoms
and sweet girl haiku

Food For Another Time

Men come here with their ATVs
and motorbikes when the river is low,
tearing deep grooves into silt
as soft as silk that clings
and grabs my boots
pulling me to another world.

Here the birds are jubilant,
bouncing boughs with their
joyous landings, new buds
waiting to unfurl.

Insects swarm my face
the closer I get to the water.
I am food for another time,
my breath is something
that feeds the trees.

I should be mad about the grooves
and the man-made intrusion
but my footprints leave no less
of a trace than the other.

I know the river will rise
and curl its waters over
the banks like a leaf butterfly
making a cocoon to hold
a week long transformation
whose mark could last a year.

The river holds secrets
like she's always done
and I find myself at her

rushing bank again,
waiting for signs
and deep understanding.

Threads
for Rebecca Schumejda

The sun shines against a blue sky,
a color I can't even describe
but takes the breath from my chest.
The wind stealthily slides around
corners of buildings to find
the delicate bare skin
of my neck left uncovered.

I'm out searching for this poem,
the universe granting me
an extra morning off work
and time is not to be wasted
on things like vacuuming or laundry.
But all that fills my ears is the sound
of traffic and conversational chatter
blending together on the sidewalk.

I've placed restrictions on these poems
like a conservative parent
who thinks they know best,
who sees the potential in you
but doesn't know the right way
to make you flourish.

The dark edges of my heart
says it is needed, that bruise
still tender like some throwback
to my childhood when standing
inside the rules meant survival.

But now, the idea of being considered
a woman with only one note
swirling around in an endless bag

of letters and words is a larger concern
than I'd ever like to admit is true.

I give up on the poem and resign to reading
the work of a decades known acquaintance,
a book filled with one long heartache
whose story the reader
has to cobble together and consider.

It is a book full of questions
without question marks,
a book looking for hard answers
and a chord strikes in the center of me.
My fear and revulsion of poems
laced with question marks
that has followed me for a lifetime,
always challenging me to give over
pieces of myself that are ugly and unseen,
boils up from the depths of me.

I cry in the middle of the coffee shop,
so hard I have to remove my glasses,
tears splattering against the inside
and the backs of my hands evolve
into meaty, makeshift tissues.

I close the book, unable to continue
and the skylight above me fills
the room with an unnatural light
like a beacon of understanding
for everything made tangible
in this expansive world.

I think about the poem I was supposed
to write, filled with sparrows and nests
and think about how her poem

is a thread I would gather to weave
into a shelter that would hold
my most precious things.
And I would sit inside singing
clear songs, the jubilant notes
rising toward the sun like ether
on bracing spring winds
and I would somehow be whole.

Descent

There is a break in the rain,
sky splitting into the kind of blue
that saves my soul
when I stare at it.

He and I lace up our boots
for an uncharted adventure.
This place is a familiar vision to me—
the park on the top of the hill
where I used to walk my dog,
where my child broke my finger with a fast pitch,
        her arm stronger than she knew,
where a boyfriend once danced
        with me under the moonlight.

These memories are decades old,
stacked on top of each other like cordwood.

Now, the cherry trees are starting to bud,
but it's been too cold for blooms.

We find an opening into the wild woods
and follow the barely visible deer trail
up and down the side of the mountain
with people's backyards to our left
and the unknown within reach of our right.

I talk about the glaciers
that pushed through here,
cutting stone and earth.
We find deer blinds and tree stands.
We find trash left by wayward teenagers.

On the descent, we are left with no choice
but to cut through someone's yard and I'm nervous.
I know the types of people who live here, who
love their second amendment.
He tells me to hold down the metal shovel
on my pack, placed there to ward off animals
and dig trenches, because even at fifty,
I'm still afraid to trespass.

Ritual of Transition

Outside the kitchen window
I watch the storm blow
the remnants of last year's leaves.
The sky spits snow and then rain,
the season is confused
in so many ways.

My knees ache
in the ritual of transition.
Youth fades from my body
as my mind gets younger
and more free.

I slice fruit and boil pasta
for a salad, prepping for a weekend
of long hours filled
with the cacophony
of hospital bells
and emotional demands.

Soon he'll be here by my side
and we'll move about the kitchen together,
keeping each other accountable for living
as long as we can, both of us stopping
in front of the window,
close and holding space
for each other, watching
our lives intertwine.

There Are Still Mountains To Climb
For Lisa

Spring is here blanketing
everything in a misty sheen.
From the highway, I can see the trees
turning their invisible outstretched
leaves to the rain, almost hear the elegant
sound the drops make as they touchdown.

A bird flies perpendicular to the hood of my car,
black and sharp, its speed a mystery to me
and I pretend it is a swallow home from the Caribbean
but it's not the right color nor the right time for migration.

But I think of her anyway, how she never touches the ground,
always running from one point to the other trying to escape
invisible monsters we both see when we close our eyes.

As soon as I arrive and we sit at a table meant for a family,
her face falls into a shadow of fear. She blurts out the worst
word in the English language and I feel a small dagger
pierce my ribs. She half cries and I sit silent, gathering it.

We move on as if nothing was ever said,
our bodies used to the reverberation of destruction,
and speak of art and love and waterfalls.

Today the hills are hazy with rain,
the river filling its banks and the grackles
take cover on the pine boughs.
I wonder if there is room enough
for us there to shelter our hearts
from the weight of it all.

Subtle Movements

I stepped out into a rain colder than I expected
on a day I chose not to layer myself
from the fickle and ever-changing elements.

I'm here because I didn't show up for myself—
the winter was an extended hibernation, or at least
I tell myself this rather than bathe
in the honesty of my depression.

I don't like the way it pulls at my skirts, how the world
drains into monochrome. It goes quiet like a French film,
the contemplation heavy and my heart even heavier.

I move forward with boots squelching
in the mud of early spring, my eyes
in search of green, of any signs that I
can still bloom after being left unattended.

On the island at the park, the geese have arrived.
By May, they will have taken over, but for now I push them back
into the water with my subtle movements.

They are tired from migration and don't even honk
their displeasure and protest.
Some part of me wants to cry at this,
some part of me understands.

Awakening

This body is a rainbow,
a spiritual ascension
at once an awakening
into emptiness
ether trapped between
sun and the absence of

like a meditation
on what it means to be.

We.

We, the children of trauma,
find our feet planted in any place
destroyed by the hands of man,
those green spaces leveled
those boggy marshes and ponds
filled with old tires and detritus.

We, the children of trauma,
sprout up like new reeds
our tightly bristled heads sway
in the wind, pollinating ourselves
for greatness, catching any breeze
filled with songs still left to sing.

We, the children of trauma,
use new feet to mark new paths
full of adventure and curiosity
reclaiming all that was stolen
from our youth that comes
looking for us now.

We, the children of trauma,
are weeds with delicate flowers
that whisper the secrets
of unknown universes.

We.

All the Empty Nests are Filled with Hope

The fog has returned to the hill
overlooking the river, the heat
from the ground still holding in
everything it stole from the sun
over the last two days, but the gray
sky and rain extract its toll.

Everything is green now that it has tasted
the sun, flowers push up from the earth
and the grackles on the line keep watch
between the trees, the alley a flurry of wings.

Soon my child will leave the house
to find her own spring, settle her roots
in a plot of land not tended by my quiet hands.
We have sat in front of the window
looking at the river, imagining if we could
see each other from our prospective perches.

She is growing older and wiser
in this march of time, yielding a crop
of thoughts like a fast growing rice field,
so much green, so much potential, so much heartache.

But for now I choose to forget about these things
and watch the small flies struggle in the spider's
yearly web nestled in the corner of the window
always reminding me of change, of the come and go,
of how things return when you think they were forgotten
and I hope my child remembers to return to me sometimes.

We Write Our Own Ending to the Story

When my child was born
I gave her a name that meant
"to bloom." My love of flowers
woven into the idea she would someday
find the strength to turn all her petals
toward the sun and be anything she wanted.

Twenty years later, we work together
to move bags and boxes into her new apartment,
all the memories we'd made together stacked
in cardboard strewn through several small rooms.
I busy myself unwrapping dishes and stacking cookbooks
thinking about the time I moved into my first home
and told my mother not to come help,
that the drive from New England was too long
and the weather, too inclement.
There was disappointment in her voice
I hadn't understood then. Maybe she knew something
I didn't, but it would've been the last time
I ever saw her alive. I robbed her of a needed moment.

This heavy tragedy catches me in my child's
new kitchen as I listen to her bustle in the next room
and feel thankful I'm allowed this opportunity
to hold her hand through another milestone.
Later, over lunch, her eyes well up like dew
collecting on the delicate petals of a complicated
peony and she tells me she never thought
she would have made it this far. I do my best
not to cry at the table, knowing four years ago
she almost didn't make it at all.

Sleeping In

The morning is filled
with pre-dawn birdsong
and the trailing calls
of the first spring peepers.

We wake up lazily,
sleep-warmed under
the covers, the room
smelling of skin
in the faint glow
of a transitional
moon/sun dance.

He touches me when
my eyes are closed
and I'm infused
with love.

This rare morning
where I am still in bed
when he wakes, when
I've allowed myself
the chance to sleep in.

His fingers make me
forget the lists in my head,
remind me that time
has never been linear
only a temporal remembrance
of how the world works.

Innocent Pride

He comes in from an evening of mowing
to tell me he's helped a struggling earthworm
cross the sidewalk. His smile is child-like,
full of innocent pride and joy at saving a life.

It brings me back to the spring nights
of my youth when a rainstorm could soak the valley
and we'd watch the worms rise up like zombies in a horror movie.
I thought it was magical. I thought they had come
to the surface to dance in the rain.

But now my mind is full of science, and I know they are refugees
from flooded burrows, that air hunger makes them risk everything,
that the rain vibrates the ground like the talons of birds
waiting to pluck them from their earthly safety.

I smile back at him, touch his warm arm damp with sweat,
at the sweet gesture of kindness and love
and keep my sharp-angled knowledge
inside my mouth and let him be a kid again.

Underground Silence

We walk down the alley, sun shining
but the wind cold enough
for him to wear long underwear.
His body still not acclimated
to the river-cooled air.

I point out flowers along the way.
It wasn't something he asked for,
but something I've given my whole life
to anyone who'll listen.
These moments allow me to be
a small girl holding
my mother's hand, imagining a world
full of leaves and petals and blooms.

As we walk past the Japanese knotweed
I tell him that bamboo only grows
to its final height and width in the first sixty days.
The rest of its life is spent inert.
He says nothing and we keep walking.
I'm still learning to be okay
with his quietness as acceptance, not rejection.

I drink this underground silence down
with a blush of the warm wind
suddenly surrounding me like
the tremble of unexpected weeping
that overcomes us when we don't fully understand why.

His warm hand finds my elbow
and slides down until our palms
face each other, our feet striking
the ground at different intervals
and I hear the internal cries
of the world around me
that I have no power to change.

Quiet Underpinnings

On spring mornings, the ones
right before summer lifts her skirt
of light, I become intoxicated
by the smell of life growing
at imperceptible rates.

The birds stuff their beaks
with twigs and fat worms
and around their full mouths
are the love songs
I've spent my entire life
trying to understand.

I think about the quiet underpinnings
of nature that we never see:

how the mulberry tree emits
a special scent like jasmine
that only silkworms can smell—the way
their bodies lift from another leaf
just to drink that elixir in further

or how they are oblivious
to the man-made plans
that get them to spin their silk
around their bodies in hopes
of becoming a lighter, more colorful
version of themselves
only to be boiled alive without
ever knowing the truth.

The sky is gray this morning
as I think of this, and the edges
of my mind grabs hold

of another mass shooting,
more children died for nothing,
all of them were silkworms
waiting to be butterflies.

Life is Improvisation

Under cosmic lights,
once bare floors
of white maple
are now covered
with scattered limbs
and colorful bodies.

Our wild minds
are plucked at random
and added to the brine
of something new
like golden petals
of safflower.

The piano fills the room
and my heart—my eyes close
feeling the spark
of heartbeats
out of time.

The minor chords strike
and his warm fingers
gently touch my Achilles heel.

I am learning to mine
his silence for the words
I can't hear.

I am learning to find him
in all the spaces
that are unexpected.

Summer's Teeth

The sun is already blaring by 9:30 am
when we step out of the car at the mouth
of an old cemetery. American flags wave
against the ancient stones, reminding me it's
Memorial Day. Sometimes, just another day.

It is the anniversary of my uncle's death,
his unfortunate suicide, but I don't realize this
until we are searching for a hiking trail
hidden in the upper edges of the rural cemetery.

The stones hold names that are familiar
after twenty years of nursing people back
to life in this community, though we always
lose some. The smell rising from wide swathes
of Lily of the Valley pulls at my heart
as memories I thought I'd forgotten bubble up.

The air is hot and dry—summer's teeth
just starting to nibble at our heels
and all of nature stretches her arms out
to pull it in close.

We peek the trail sweating as it opens
to a large clearing. An air strip is neatly
mowed down the center and in the distance
a stand of tall pines sway in the breeze.

The morning's meditation comes back to me—
a soft voice saying I'd emerge from a forest
into a vast clearing. I did it backwards
and laugh at how truly fitting this is.

We push on, our conversation sprinkled
with gene keys and how life is wound so
tightly that we sometimes forget how to live,
but not out here. Nature unspools us, lets us
breathe more deeply into the people
we'd always hoped we would be.

At the bottom of the valley we find
a small waterfall and an overlook
where someone got married, but abandoned
their wedding arbor. We stood under it
together—this man-made thing
gathered from forest floor and scraps
of love and for a moment, the fear
of being unlovable leaves me.

On the drive home, with the hot air
cooling the sweat on our skin, we watch
the thresher taking down the first hay and wheat
and let the space around us linger
with a silence so bright, we can't speak.

I'll Meet You At The River

Words fall out of my mouth
in a sharp litany, and I want them
back as soon as they've left
the perch of my dry tongue.
The evidence of my anxiety
is no longer a secret tucked
under my warm, fleshy arm
or hidden in the red origami box
on my desk that is barely
strong enough to hold air.

I watch the darkest part of me
emerge before him from an ootheca
like a thousand colorless nymphs—
all those infant mantis tumbling wingless
onto the earth, clinging to each others backs,
None of them have learned what praying
is all about while waiting there
to eat each other up without thought.

He finally pushes back against the low
roar of my demands and unending list of rules,
tearing the brittle foam casing from around
my mouth until there is nothing but shreds
of silence from both of us. The pressure
created is more than my heart can stand
so I sit on the porch alone trying to figure out
where my anger comes from and why
it surfaces without warning or reason.

Outside, the rain taps gently against the window,
as the road grows more slick and shiny.

Fear is the only thought to rise—being afraid
is the well from which my water rises:

afraid of things out of my control
afraid of goodness and love
afraid of time stealing the best parts of me
afraid of distance swallowing the rest

and when everything is too quiet,
he asks if I want to go rock hunting
knowing the river will find me lighter,
that the sound of the water might remind me
of what we are traveling toward
instead of keeping us swimming
in a shallow eddy with what we've
been running from our entire lives.

And for a moment,
we both can breathe.

He kisses my cheek and holds my hand,
the warmth of him always a surprise
and everything inside me that's held
together with elementary school glue
and macaroni bandages, begins
to soften and melt, waiting to be born
into this moment of giving.

I Still Keep Reaching

It's been over a week
since we've seen each other's faces
without work looming on the other side,
without responsibility pulling
at the spaces we find hardest to let go.
We've known the taste of hunger.
It's tattooed inside our mouths.

It's been over a week since
he's held my face like
I was precious porcelain
or a fragile beam of light.

It's been over a week since
we've held hands in the darkness
making up stories about far worlds
and impossible adventures
and the nonsense childish imagination.

It's been over a week since
I've whispered secrets into
the crevasse of his chest
where a rib was once taken
in hopes his breath would be put back
to its rightful place.

He does not know
that all the birds sitting on wires
        or the ones pulling worms in the yard
        are my father's soul come to visit
or how his ghost feeds on the heart
        of my love to help me write poems.

I forget to tell him about the fireflies
        and how they need long grass to hide
away from the sun or how our human
encroachment dampens the light
from their tiny bodies by leaving no
dark spaces for them to shine,

or how their fleeting glow is a mating ritual
or how as a child I was mesmerized by this light,
        this magical thing that was beyond my reach
but I still kept reaching for it. That wonderment
        so powerful it would surround me in a field
        and I would feel separated
        from the world
        for just a moment.

It's been a week since
we've seen each other's faces
and the secrets of the world
are stacking up in my mouth
like cordwood waiting
to be set on fire.

Never Get Old

The heat grips me as I climb the hill,
a bag full of discs slung on my back
and me chasing away the pains in my body
with sheer will as I step closer and closer to forty-nine.
At the top, I'm dizzy with probable dehydration
and the fact that my body hasn't retained the agility
it once had—like those days I rode bareback on horses
in the summer heat, the sun a fireball in the cloudless sky,
the desert so full of space and imagination that my mind
would empty out behind me and get tangled in the horse's tail.

What a body could endure then, thighs gripping
the muscular frame of the horse, the rock and jolt
of my bones when I'd push him to full gallop,
one hand tight on the reins and the other on a paper bag
full of dried salted plums. I used to think of the fruit's life cycle,
juicy flesh left in the blaze of the sun to dry and shrivel,
how its surface reminded me of old women baked
in the heat of summer. The salt of their tears was alive
in my mouth, made it water and let me forget
I was thirsty, that I could die out there.

The others tell me it's my turn to shoot, the memory fades
into the humidity of the afternoon and I haul my aged body
to the tee trying to bring back the youth of those desert mornings
when no one cared where we were or who we were,
where life was just something that happened
under pale blue sky and over cracked earth split by hooves.
There was freedom in the illusion that I'd never get old,
that nothing would ever steal the innocence of that moment.

Kiss Me When You Get Home

The nights when he works I pace inside my skull
until I have to fill my eyes with videos of dancers
or boyish mediums connecting famous people
with their dead loved ones. It fascinates me the way
their tears fall just as easily as my own from messages
beyond the grave that were not meant for me.

I never imagined that the empty side of the bed
would steal sleep from me when for so many years
it did the opposite when filled. It's a feeling like floating
low over an open meadow, not quite close enough
to earth, not quite high enough to say I'm flying.

My fingertips graze over the delicate lavender petals
of self-heal wishing they were strong enough
for me to anchor myself there and fix all the open
wounds that still exist from another time.
The thought makes me sleepy but my mind won't let go.

I settle for thunderstorms on loop
and the faint hot glow of my screen
upside down on the nightstand.

The pocket door slides noisily when he comes to bed,
my body rising with some unseen force to wrap
my arms around his shower-warmed body.
The smell of him is so sweet and clean.
My body melts into the strength of his arms
and some part of this release scares me.
This love more different than anything before
that leaves me independent and headstrong
and wanting just a little bit more than seems fair.

Summer Violet

We stand together, a community gathered,
lifting voices and arms into a sky
blushing in summer violet.
This act of standing up for each other,
for myself, a new and challenging experience
leaving my head dizzy and heart racing
at what it means to belong
to more than a whispered illusion.

I close my eyes to the crowd around me,
my imagination unfurling each one of us
into brilliant irises painted in hues
of purple, the color of feminism,
the final arc in the rainbow
where a goddess was rumored
to have spoken across all time
and space, the secrets of this world.

When I open my eyes, I'm merely human.
A woman with her best friend
on one side, her child on the other,
understanding for once in my life
the power of a village and the strength
of too many women scorned.

Sitting on the Curb, Independence Day

Our independence comes with a price,
freedoms get taken for granted
and exploited on hot summer days
when people gather to remember
their youth, more than the birth
of a nation. They gather to remember
a time when independence was picnics
and parades, ice cream and marching bands,
flags and the feeling of time standing still
amongst the fireflies and roman candles.

Now we sit paralyzed, the crow dipper
strangling us with its poison, keeping
us low to the ground and hypervigilant
like wild animals and small children
waiting for the next random shooting
on a beautiful day. There is no way
to make it stop. No way to wipe the
phrase "this doesn't happen here" from
our trembling lips. No way to wash
the blood off of Main Street USA.
No way to piece back together
the stories our grandparents told us
that made us believe
in the possibility
of forever.

Between the Lines We Find a Glimpse of Truth

We push through a wall of cold air
before the sliding doors open
and crash into waves of hot, July heat.
He and I catch our breath in the transition
as I park his wheelchair and wait
for his wife to bring the car.

He points out to the landscaping
and says much of this is his handiwork
and I nod in amazement.
At 70, I'd think the work too much
and it brings me back to my days in Atlanta
working landscaping for a man
who thought less of women,
and gave me all the worst jobs
just to taste the joy of seeing me quit.

I slaved in the hot sun, dehydrated
while edging large lots, getting laughed at
by young men shaped in southern,
unspoken laws of caste and culture—
their fathers approving of a woman's
place being in the kitchen.

The boss placed me on a stand up mower
that no one taught me to drive, and told me
to suck it up each of the times
I held back waves of vomit
while spraying deadly weed killer
to keep a rich man's lawn pristine
and hoped I didn't get cancer.

I tell him about the job, but only the part
that recognizes how hard the work is
and how I can't believe he's still doing it.

He tells me he had to use up
all his vacation time for surgery
or he'd lose his job and how his boss
was mad that he was not going to be part
of the workforce with the upcoming
heavy summer load.

I realized then that I didn't have to share
the part about being mistreated
as he was already familiar, and for this,
I wanted to hug him for being made to feel
like his life was expendable at the sake
of padding someone else's pockets.

We waited in silence for his wife
to pull the car around,
enjoying the air and the sun,
and all the memories
we were not likely to forget.

The Mystery of Her Smile

All day I felt the gnawing
of my grandmother's death.

Four years gone and each day
is still a mystery that misses
the quiet comfort of her smile

that always reminded me
of a lotus blooming in the mud,
how her life had handed her
struggle and hardship, abuse,

and how she faced it with a strength
that never challenged authority
yet was stronger than any baton
or hand raised to push her down.
When they called me that afternoon

and said they'd found her face down
in the threshold of her doorway,
groceries stacked on the porch
with her head by the dining table, heavy
winter coat wrapped around her soul
keeping her from the snow flying

through the screen door parted by her small boots,
I almost collapsed on the pavement.
Now, the dark of the room surrounds me, the whir
of the AC and the racing of my own heart
are the only soundtracks I have left.

My tears find their way down my
cheeks, drying in the false chill
as fast as I can produce them,

and I stay as quiet as a mouse
save the escaped shudder
of my ribs against the mattress.

I feel his warm hand against my back
and he asks what's wrong. I tell him
she would've been 89. He asks me
to tell him a good story about her
making me fall in love with him all over again.

No Hesitation

Everyday from my living room
I watch the sun rise, blushing
behind the hills on the other side
of the river. There, my child is still
asleep, in the nest of her own making.

Like a mother hawk I'm perched
at a distance, waiting and watching,
as fledgling wings open wide
and flap, lifting her feet only inches
from the branch. Life is hard,
even harder knowing from experience
the darkness that lurks around corners.

I did not hesitate to leave when it was my turn.
I flew hard and fast, spiraled through
the air, but landed every time, on my feet.
Did my mother worry about me
like I worry about my child?
It's something I'll never know.
But my worry is palpable,
even from this distance,
as I imagine them waving goodbye
just beyond the edge of the trees.

Manipulating Time

I think of the Paulownia tree,
something I've never seen before
and can only imagine
with its voluminous purple flowers
shaped like foxglove, leaves
like a million small umbrellas.

I think of how in winter
the heavy limbs freeze
and drop but grow more readily.
It's as if it is trying to outgrow itself,
trying to stay ahead of time.
Humans aren't much different,
this need to gather and manipulate
something we only think we can quantify
with science and math.

I think about him gone from here
only 24 hours and how my heart beats
so hard I feel my own limbs could drop.
This is fear, in part, the hoping
he'll not find something better on his journey.
But mostly it is love, so profound
and deep that I barely understand it.

Somewhere in Japan, the countryside
smells of vanilla. Here, I begin to bake.
This is my tree. This is my attempt
to manipulate time until he returns.

The Kind of Summer

The rains come in from the west
and here, we are always getting
the rags of someone else's weather
siphoning through our valley.

It washes away the humidity
leaving a week's worth of perfect
summer, the kind I remember
as a child before global warming
became our everyday weather.

The kind of summer where I reach
for a sweatshirt.

The kind of summer where all
the windows get left open.

The kind of summer that smells
of fresh cut hay on country roads.

The kind of summer where fireflies
hover in the yard at dusk.

The kind of summer that makes me
want to dance barefoot in the grass
to feel the damp earth cradling
the soles of my feet.

I cherish these remembrances
knowing they are fleeting, that
next week the air will be so thick
and hazy that I won't be able to breathe,
or that my skin will be set on fire
from the porch to the car.

All the Secrets

The air is humid and heavy
as if the rains are not far off.
A haze filters over the hills,
the distance, much like the future
of the world, is muted and gray.
But the present is filled
with the ghost of Samuel Clemens.

The rich sloping lawn, verdant
and alive with the sound of crickets,
the faint buzzing of bees
lazily moving from clover to clover.
Paperwhites hover low,
their life seemingly aimless
while the birds chitter and chirp
to each other in a language
I've yet to decipher.

The breeze asks me questions
I have no answers for, though,
part of me wonders if they are tucked
in the crevices of the slate stone fence
running the length of the property.
They remind me of my grandmother's house,
of all the secrets I've tucked into dark places
among the moss and exoskeletons
of insects past their prime.

I'm not sure why I'm here
I only know that I'm waiting
for the rains to wash me clean.

Disconnected

I woke in the night
to winds clattering
the garbage can,
to rain pelting
the air conditioner
that probably doesn't
need to be running.

The winds shake me awake again
howling as they get stuck
on the angles of the house's addition.

In the morning, I learn
there was a tornado watch
and realize this is how
disconnected from reality
I've become since the pandemic.

We could have died,
I think.
But we didn't,
I say aloud.

We Will Teach Each Other

I came home after twelve hours of office sterility
to find him covered in sawdust from head to toe
with a childish smile across his face,
a rarity I've come to love.

Pieces of wood were laid out on an old door,
the rough translation of a new art piece.
He's trying to envision the creation in his heart.
Words escape him as he tries to explain it.
His visions are not my visions.

We stand eating store-bought sandwiches,
the summer evening humidity starting to dissipate
and the bugs beginning their ritual melody
that adds to my drowsiness.

Together we finish tightening the wire
on our trellis garden, nothing more
than laundry posts repurposed
and he waits for my direction.

I begin working with thin bamboo rods
staking
tying
speaking
wishes to the plants.

He cuts small lengths for cross bars,
holds them still while I fumble
tying them together in the heavy dusk.
The pale blue sky is threaded with wisps
of gray clouds and apricot sunset.

When it's done he admits he thought
it was going to be a terrible construction,
that he should have trusted my vision.
It is this we will teach each other
under the watchful eyes of the sky
and the sweet song of crickets.

Glowing Eyes

Every morning I leave
before the sun remembers
It's alive with light
and cosmic energy.

The mornings are engulfed
by fog so thick it feels
full of ghosts holding hands—
the front of my car
shattering connections.

It's hard to see deer this way
but my eyes dart anyway,
hoping to see their glowing
eyes peering through.

I listen to my book
like a mantra
steeling myself
for what the day
might bring me
if I make it there
alive.

Dragonflies

We sit in the campground waiting
for the concert gates to open,
hundreds of tents crammed together
without regard to space.

The air is thick with humidity,
my skin and clothes damp
to the touch doing nothing
but existing. I can feel the rain
lurking over the hillside.

I lean back in my chair
trying to block out
the conversations around me,
tilt my head to the darkening sky.
There, I see dozens of green
dragonflies darting and floating
through the sky.

It reminds me of the cottonwood
trees when they release their lint,
how it is everywhere and nowhere
at the same time.

It reminds me of my mother,
the way the dragonfly hovers
and disappears. I wish she
would have stayed longer.

The Memory of Summer

The sun fades earlier
but forgets to take its heat
with it, thickness hangs
in the air as dusk winds
its spindly purple fingers
over everything.

In bed, I lie there awake
in the oppression despite
air conditioning and try
to remember summers
when the nights were
so cool I needed a sweatshirt
to keep the chill out of my bones.

But we live in different times,
the seasons dragging the last
one behind later and later
until I have to give up on
the meaning of time.

Where The Mud Opens Up to the River

We give up walking at the river's edge,
the rains thoroughly soaking the banks
into a makeshift marshland,
into imaginary rice fields emerging
from the unending green backdrop of the hills.

The universe is more alive
than we give it credit for,
more alive that we can see
with necks stooped and faces
awash in mesmerizing blue light.

We leave the manicured path
where the mud opens up to the river
and stand there holding hands.
Traffic buzzes on the highway above us—
the clacking of the train calls
to all the parts of our souls
that always want to keep moving.

The river does just that—moves forward
moving, moving, moving.

He kisses me on the neck
just to hear me laugh
and it echoes inside my head—
this whisper of silent freedom
we've granted each other,
this open field of green
in which we grow every day.

Warm Air Rising

I stand on the sidewalk,
my body shifting backward
to compensate for the decline,
and look out over the yard.

The pre-dawn fog has come
nearly every day, some days
so thick and heavy it looks
like snow clinging to the long
blades of grass that beg to be cut.

I think about its formation,
warm air rising, earth cooling
and moisture trapped
in the space between.
There is something quiet
and unsettling about it today.

I make myself get into the car
to drive to work, eyes wide
and searching for creatures
in the mist.

Harbingers of Rain

We walk through the forest,
the fall day is warmer
than expected. We planned
on only walking out to look
at the expansive gorge
and beautiful waterfall,
but went deeper and deeper,
following the winding trail.

It descended steeply
and here I remember
we have no water
as my heartbeat quickens,
but I tell myself I'll be okay.

These white lies sometimes
necessary to keep going.
By the time we hike back up,
I am not alright.
Heat exhausted and dizzy,
I lay on the cold stone fence
embraced by the shade.

I think I hear the beautiful song
of the white wagtail, these gracious
birds whose fluttering tails are said
to make them harbingers of rain.
But I know they do not migrate here—
the distance too far.

I am left with the knowledge
I'm hallucinating in the heat
and cling to the rocks
for reality.

Humanness

"I was a mother. I was a wife. I had a mind."—Kate Hansen Fowler

These thoughts leave my mind
like the last remaining swallows
finding their way home
from North America to South.
They turn themselves over to the heat
and what is left of the season
in this part of the country.

I talk to a friend about the vacancy
a mother feels when they try to remember
who they are outside the realm
of mother
of wife
inside the confines of a mind
once full of ideas and curiosity.

We volley the idea of definitions
handed down by generations
that try to define us as individuals
with generic labels—as if this will
make us feel like we belong
to a greater community.
In middle age, we are still struggling
to figure out who we are
without these procured definitions.

All of this happens simultaneously
to a conversation with my adult child
where I find myself admitting
I was once so lost in those definitions
that it nearly drove me to suicide.

The erasure of identity was more
than I thought I could live with
but when she was a child, her tiny hand
upon my cheek, asking me to eat waffles with her
on the couch and watch cartoons, saved my life.

Sometimes it's hard to admit my humanness.
It feels like weakness and failure.
It feels like giving up and standing up
at the same time. But I show my imperfections
anyway, because at this point,
I don't know what else to do.

The Silence of Easiness

I step into a cacophony of bird song,
the loudest thing I've heard all day
trapped inside the confines of comfort,
the silence of easiness.

As I step away there is a great hush
like thunder lowering its voice.
What is left is the wind moving through
the tops of trees and the beating of my heart in my ears.

This Age of Spontaneous Combustion

It's hibernation time,
I feel it in my bones
but nature's not fully
reflecting the season.

Afternoons are dark and damp.
Humidity lifting up its fists laughing,
no sweaters yet for me,
not in this age of spontaneous combustion,
this unregulated body of emotions and temperatures.

I watch apples roll downhill,
striking the raised beds
full of aging vegetables,
bouncing like rubber balls
into the construction workers
freshly-dug holes in the sidewalk.

It's all dying—the tomatoes,
the basil bolting and full of busy bees,
the squash offering one last fruit.

Winter's coming, I say laughing
to myself. The world is one big meme
stuck to the insides of my eyelids,
but I feel this change with certainty.

Banging on the Door

I stand in the cool air
banging on the red door
waiting to be acknowledged
in some small way.

Rage fills me up from toes
to crown, my heart beating
like a machine gun over
a draining rice paddy
in a long forgotten war.

I feel alone, abandoned
by the person I love most,
the sensation reaching back
decades until my fist
appears small and plump.

Had I not been doing this
all my life? Banging on
a secret door inside
my heart, waiting for
someone to tell me
they'd been expecting me.

Hope Lake

I stare out over Hope Lake,
the sun lighting up the burnt leaves
of trees against the pale blue sky.

Again this sky reflecting back
the color of my mother's eyes.

Again with me looking into them
searching for answers.

Chevrons of geese merge
into a tornado of feathers,
spinning slow and methodical,
all of them reaching down
to the placid lake.

Silent House

The sun rises quietly
behind banks of clouds
leftover from yesterdays
consistent rain.

There are breaks
in the darkness,
pale blue patches
like individual petals
of the Chrysanthemum.

The sight fills me
with joy in the silent
house with one cat
rubbing against
my bare ankles.

This
is my favorite
type of morning.

A Future Promise

Covered in dirt, sweat beading behind
my ears, I think of how the weather
is changing. Mid-October and my body
rages about the heat, but my mind
settles into soaking up the sun.

I kneel, measuring lines in the dirt,
my Korean hand plow slicing
a furrow down the long bed
from end to end in satisfaction.
I pull the first clove of garlic
from the paper bag and push
it into the earth. A future promise.

Grasshoppers sing their song
hiding in the long grass still
needing to be mowed. I hear them
hiding in the dying hosta, and
the ornamental grasses that
have started to droop.

When all the rows are planted,
I stand with stiff back and knees
to survey the valley below me full
of everything that is important to me—
family, friends, community, the hills
and the river. This life I have built
from the seed of knowing will
someday hold me
as I lie dying.

The Rich Stuff

At the window in the morning,
I sip hot coffee looking out at the garden
covered in a layer of thin frost.
I shouldn't be disappointed
as it's almost November but some part
of me knows what will come
when the sun goes to sleep
and all I am left with is her dull
blanket of grey spread across everything.

We put on our dirt clothes and load shovels
into the back of the truck. It is the opening
day of fall dirt and we have beds to fill, plans
to make in our heads for the next season.

We are the first ones there, my man and I
smile at each other, like we were the first ones
to One-Eyed Willy's rich stuff, and just maybe
we are. For the next twenty minutes, all I hear
is the sound of our shovels hitting dirt, the twist
and lift before we throw it like dreams into the
ether. Our breaths mingled with small talk
with neighbors we don't know but who know
our gardens. I sip water and move a hair
off the bridge of my nose

As blue sky peeks through the grey,
and I lean on my shovel soaking up
the last tendrils of autumn. Winter is in
the air, the cut of the river winds and the hint
of the smell of snow in the air. I keep shoveling
until there is no more room left, until my shoulders
sing a sad song of their own.

The Flaw

My best girlfriend and I walk on the bright
side of the street, hoping what little sun
there is will warm our heavy bones.

We walk and talk, catching up on each other's
writing careers, the mental health of our children,
how getting older has its wisdom, but the health
issues get more baffling with each new day.

Up and down the street we move quickly
dodging pedestrians, waiting for cars,
leaning into the next topic that flows
from one mouth or the other.

On the last lap we know it is really the last one,
far off in the distance rain clouds move slowly
but with intent and neither of us are willing
to put up with it if we don't have to.

I always want to hug her goodbye, but she
doesn't like to be hugged. Maybe it is the one
flaw in our friendship, the chink in our proverbial
armor.

Unexpected

The universe pushes me hardest
when the leaves of the maple
turn faded yellow and cling
to the bottom branches, as if
to tell me to never give up,
to keep pushing through
the darkness. It whispers
of spring and new ivy, delicate
as it unfurls with evening song.

The world is good. I feel this,
at least here in this place,
where friends still meet
for plays and the sky still
turns a blushed pink
in the most unexpected ways.

The Truth of Everything

Somewhere in the world
the camellia is beginning
to bud, unfurling like a
bloom of blood in the water.

Here, my own heart
is forming in the dappled
shade of autumn, under
layers of fog and streetlight.

My small hand reaches out
like a petal from the calyx,
reaching for everything
I've missed in life.

How strong am I?
Can I find the light?
When will I see
the truth of everything?

Until My Breath is No More

My body is beginning
to freeze, to turn down
the dial on living.

Outside the winds blow,
inside I shed blood
and fears.

I remember a prayer
and dedicate myself
to say it.

Fire On The Mountain

On the hill across the river
a light glows like the center
of a newly flowered daffodil.

The air speaks spring but it is
nothing more than a lie
I long to hear, again and again.

The light wavers and without
my glasses, my heart tells me
the hill will catch fire.

I wait and watch, contemplate
why I had never noticed
this before. I watch trucks

pass on the highway, wait
for the light to flicker when
they race past, but it stays still.

Does my heart wish for fire?
For destruction and rebirth?
I cannot say for sure and go back

to writing my simple life
onto the pages no one
will ever read.

Friendsgiving

The sky is full of gray, sullen ideas
and I wait inside an empty room
for strangers to arrive.

A rainbow of personalities
file through the door,
but I am distracted

by the brilliant red
of a maple sapling
in the backyard.

The house is suddenly filled
with laughter and stories, voices
from every walk of life.

I move into the center of it,
a grand table filled with people
and food to share,

It is a circle of greatness
and I feel more blessed
than I have in a long time.

Almost enough
to forget it is
my father's birthday.

Quiet Optimism

We leave the poetry reading,
nothing more than a palm full
of friends sharing their hearts
and painful truths. I love the
collective sigh when a line strikes
the bubble of acknowledgement
that sits at the back of the throat,
knowing he's found pieces
to his awkward, but growing tribe.

There is something cheerful
about his quiet optimism
as we leave the bookstore,
a trait I'm sure he's
never acknowledged exists
in the likes of his body,
but I feel it there
until we leave the shelter
of the bricks and mortar
that built this town
hundreds of years ago.

The north winds rustle
the giant Christmas tree
in the square, and I feel him shiver
where our arms are looped together.

His sweet confidence from earlier,
when the air was too warm for winter,
fails him as he remembers how the north
does its business, always full of surprises.

I offer him my warm coat
and like a gentleman he refuses
so I hold him a little tighter
happy to be alive with him.

The Shift

It's December and the weather
is balmy like the beginning of spring.
My heart aches a little knowing
the earth is changing in the wrong
direction, knowing that someday
the post-apocalypse movies
of my childhood could come true.

It bothers me enough to find my way
to the creek, the need to hear the water
feels sharp inside me, the desire real.

The banks are muddy from the morning rains,
the smell of pine and cedar fresh as it mixes
with the decay of autumn, not yet gone.

Flowers stand like hollow ghosts
their pale white petals a reminder
of their youth, when they were
filled with the color of the sun and life.

Somewhere on the hill there
is a campfire. Its smoke filling me
with memories. Overhead, three crows fly,
one calling out as it falls behind.
There is a moment when the vapor
of my warm breath mixes with the drifting smoke
and I am not sure if my feet
are touching the ground.

Monochrome

Winter has settled in with
imperceptible sunrises that leak
a lighter shade of gray into
the ink of night.

My body forgets what it's supposed
to do—my mind muddled in monochrome.
A thirst for color exists, clawing its way out,
a low thrum felt in the chest, the disgust
that breathes in the waiting, palpable.

What does nature tell me? Why do I
never listen to the earth's heartbeat
slow and slacken? I fight against this time
of rest only to lose. I fill my body
with false prophets and prayers
while I wait for the sun.

As Snow

Like a bear retreating to its den
to fend off the barren winter, so has
the sun taken leave from the sky.
In its wake, I'm left the dead gray
dreams of ghosts.

I let my body move forward—
every articulation screaming
a different language, none of which
I am proficient enough to understand.

There has to be some key to life here,
the way time moves through
the foreign lands of my own body
and how my mind is just as clueless as the rest.

My mother's voice whispers in my ear,
a taunting of how I am too serious,
but she wasn't wrong. She always
thought I needed to live more,
though what she really wanted
was for her own haphazard life to be justified.

I sit now in an empty gallery
with memories of her lingering—
the sounds above me filled
with the scamper of children's feet
moving between gingerbread houses,
their anticipation of Christmas ripe in the air.

But here in this room, I stare at Frida
and the glory of her confidence,
the delicate, tiny hands that created
paintings to make me weep.

There is part of me that wishes
I had her courage and the ability
to let the outside world go, to let
the projections evaporate
into the winter sky
and come back to me
as snow.

Holding Space

We meet as women, as equals
amidst the plants and animals,
the rain pelting the earth
in a strange warm winter cleansing.

We are only days from the solstice,
its energy felt, but not spoken of aloud.
Each of us preparing to swim upriver
to find the transparent edges of our souls.

We hold space here. Some of us
still learning the power of our voices,
our femininity, our connection
to the universe.

We hold space here
for all those who never
felt the earth shake
as their feet
touched the ground.

Self-Heal

I wake in the middle of winter
to the feeling of spring, pale
blue skies draped with thin
clouds, almost transparent
and the yard is lush green.

My heart opens to possibility here,
visions of self-heal pushing up
through the earth with its
delicate purple flowers,
sending a message.

As the hills lighten with sunshine
the warmth of this day reminds me
to heal myself, to find the gratitude
lingering in moments like a secret,
to spread my fingers wide
and stir the air with wonder.

Balance

At the end
of the breeding season

the biggest elk, antlers
in a majestic rack,

loses his power among
men, bones withering,
detached

now he is the same
as the young buck,
fawn, and doe.

The earth
finds her
balance.

Unpredictable

The weatherman promised us snow,
a blanket of white that before dawn
seems like magic.

The purity of crystals upon crystals—
each flake an individual, speaks
to me of evolution and life cycles.

Beneath the earth, fields
of winter wheat wait.
Hearts trembling, waiting.
Waiting for the magic
of winter to set them
on a journey.

But the earth is not as kind
as she once was, not so
predictable. The sun's warmth
delays tradition and steals
our sense of knowing.

The Creek

The first snow of winter
floats through the air,
flakes land like freckles
on my cheeks, some reminder
of a youthful face
before melting into invisibility.

Our boots make no sound,
the snow soft and forgiving
as we make our way to the creek.
My body and mind hungry
for the sound of water
to wash clean the week.

He is bundled warm within
every piece of clothing he has,
and is only out here because
he loves me, knowing his mood
will elevate when mine does.

I climb over the piles
of snow covered dirt and rocks,
the footing treacherous on clear days
and he stays behind. Once over,
I can see the creek dressed in white,
the water running to some
unknown place like the rest of us.

I step closer, mesmerized by the sight
without paying attention to feet and body.
Beneath the snow, lives a small river of ice
and I lose my pride to gravity.

On the ground, I'm face to face
with the dead man's fingers, hemlock,
a fall one foot over is one I'd never
return from. I lay there a moment
with snow trying to bury my existence
and take stock of my half-century bones.
None broken, so I get up.

Over the mound of dirt, my lover
saw nothing, knows not how the child
in me nearly killed me. I admit
the fall and he helps me back,
glasses fogged from the heat of his body,
and without hesitation, holds my hand
all the way home.

Creature of Habit

There is some grace
in warm winter days,
even when the sun
only pretends to shine
behind thick banks of gray clouds.

It's enough to know it's still here
when it throws a random blade
of light across the floor—powerful
enough to move the cat
from his perch, his body a cleft
of music, to lay in its muted warmth.

Outside the air speaks of spring
with the weight of water heavy
in my lungs, still cold enough
to remember we are leaning
back into winter. But people still
come out in colorful clothes,
their hope and desire for spring
days, excitedly palpable.

My body is heavy still
with the sadness of winter
as its dark mouth leans over
my shoulder to whisper in my ear.
He knows I'm a creature of habit,
knows I slide more easily
into shallow waters, but today,

I resist.

There are more bricks for my feet
to cover, more happenstance
smiles to steal from strangers,
and the hope of the sun to hold.

The Future in a Drop of Dew

The world is shifting.
We are some degrees off
and nature has ruffled skirts.

There is snow in Texas, wildfires
in California and for the rest of us,
a polar vortex.

It is dawn and I wait for
the pheasants first call
but hear nothing.

Snowflakes gently fall, the river
is frozen for the first time
in a long time and I wonder

if Shibukawa Shunkai knew
how much the universe would
fall off its axis from 1685 until now.

Did he see the future inside
a drop of dew or in the web
of a spider?

Could he imagine a life so far
outside the one he was living
to know what words to impart?

This is not for me to say.
I am only a soul inside this body
watching the world happen
without control or decision.

A Pain So Deep

I meet my child for breakfast.
The weather unforgiving,
a piercing negative seven
pushing its way through me
with each gust of wind.

We talk about our upcoming
journey to the sun, to the land
where the dirt will turn you
into glass, the heat of it
meant to overwhelm, to clean you.

We part ways, her to work
and me to the gym.

I ride the bike going nowhere
thinking about all the emotional
binding in my life—the efforts to try and heal
body and soul, creeping visions
of past lovers who tried to bury me,
my mother's death anniversary.

Eleven years ago she was plucked
from the earth. A pain in me so deep
I felt I'd never understand it. Every time
I thought I had escaped the grief
it wound around me like a giant
butterbur, its roots entangling my feet
holding me in one place, making me
feel her death over and over again.

The miles get longer on the bike
and sweat pours from my skin,
my old knees begin to ache
but I keep going, trying to outrun
what is always with me.

Accumulate

Anchor ice clings to the rocks
yet submerged roots accumulate
and grow like a small underwater
city, a secret place in time.

Around me the world is falling
apart, the air frozen and hard
to breathe. It's a constant
reminder of being alive.

I stare at the rocks in the creek.
They are the foundation of my
beliefs, the constant, the forever
in a time of fleeting compassion.

I want to put them in my pockets
and let their ancient wisdom
bury me back into the earth,
transform me into something whole.

Outstretched Hand

I arrive in Arizona
the warmth allowing
me to molt my old life,
shedding dark feathers
and allowing the new
to grow. I preen them
in the sun that is supposed
to be poison to me.

I begin to understand
that eggs form inside me
like new ideas, like life.

I let go of the past.
I let go of the fear.
I let go of the worry.

Here is a new idea,
my hands outstretched
to the sun like an offering.

I will grow.
I will be.
I will see.

Publication Notes

"Innocent Pride" appeared in the Community Foundation Calendar 2022

"Quiet Underpinnings" in *Poems for All*

Aleathia Drehmer spends a lot of time thinking up new challenges for herself when writing poetry, but mostly, you can find her gardening, making fire cider and herbal teas, and messing around with astrology. She is the co-editor of *Brian Fugett: Poems* (Citizens for Decent Literature Press). Aleathia is the author of seven chapbooks and currently has four collections of poetry available: *Little Graveyards* (Roadside Press), *We Don't Get to Write the Ending* (Roadside Press), *Looking for Wild Things* (Impspired), and *Layers of Half-Sung Hymns* (Cajun Mutt Press). You can follow Aleathia's journey at www.aleathiadrehmer.com.

MORE ROADSIDE PRESS TITLES

By Plane, Train or Coincidence
Michele McDannold

Prying
Jack Micheline, Charles Bukowski
and Catfish McDaris

Wolf Whistles Behind the Dumpster
Dan Provost

*Busking Blues: Recollections of a Chicago
Street Musician and Squatter*
Westley Heine

Unknowable Things
Kerry Trautman

How to Play House
Heather Dorn

Kiss the Heathens
Ryan Quinn Flanagan

St. James Infirmary
Steven Meloan

Street Corner Spirits
Westley Heine

*A Room Above a
Convenience Store*
William Taylor Jr.

Resurrection Song
George Wallace

*Nothing and Too Much
to Talk About*
Nancy Patrice Davenport

*Bar Guide for the
Seriously Deranged*
Alan Catlin

Born on Good Friday
Nathan Graziano

Under Normal Conditions
Karl Koweski

The Dead and the Desperate
Dan Denton

Clown Gravy
Misti Rainwater-Lites

Walking Away
Michael D. Grover

All in a Pretty Little Row
Dan Provost

*These Are the People in
Your Neighbourhood*
Jordan Trethewey

*They Said I Wasn't
College Material*
Scot Young

Radio Water
Francine Witte

*And Blackberries
Grew Wild*
Susan Mickelberry

Licorice Heart
Miles Budimir

Disposable Darlings
Todd Cirillo

Full Moon Midnight
Belinda Subraman

More Roadside Press Titles

Innocent Postcards
John Pietaro

Cistern Latitudes
James Duncan

*Another Saturday Night
in Jukebox Hell*
Alan Catlin

Abandoned By All Things
Karl Koweski

Ain't These Sorrows Sweet?
Lauren Scharhag

*Gregory Corso:
Ten Times a Poet*
Edited by Leon Horton

*She Throws Herself Forward
to Stop the Fall*
Dave Newman

*We Don't Get to
Write the Ending*
Aleathia Drehmer

*These Many Cold
Winters of the Heart*
Ryan Quinn Flanagan

*Things You Never
Knew Existed*
Josh Olsen

Maze
Jennifer Juneau

*Green Roses Bloom
for Icarus*
Hiromi Yoshida

Let the Scaffolds Fall
Shaun Rouser

Apocalypsing
Jason Anderson

Failing to Fall
James Griffin

Last Bacchanale
George Wallace

Thrift Store Jackets
Karl Koweski

Night Bird Flying
Danny Shot

*All Skate: True Stories
from Middle Life*
Lori Jakiela

*Cloud Watching
in the Inferno*
Westley Heine

Current Disasters
Jen McConnell

*Better Than The
Best American Poetry*
Dave Newman

Little Graveyards
Aleathia Drehmer

The Screw City Poems
Richard Vargas

*and all of us drinking
the blood of our enemies*
John Sweet

MORE ROADSIDE PRESS TITLES

This Is Where We Are
Nicholas Claro

With Her Hair on Fire
Christy Prahl

Perseverance:
The Making of
a Musician
Steven Grey

Fatherless Children
Michael D. Grover

A Better Loser
Nathan Graziano

The People Are Like
Wolves to Me
William Taylor Jr.

Collected Poems
(2005-2025)
Michele McDannold

The Work Anxiety Poems
Alan Catlin

Nowhere to Go but Everywhere:
Travel Poems
Milenko 'Miles' Budimir

www.ingramcontent.com/pod-product-compliance
Lightning Source LLC
Chambersburg PA
CBHW030605130626
46552CB00006B/2666

9 7 9 8 9 9 9 6 2 5 6 6 3